D0946501

Natural Disasters

Earthquakes

Andrea Rivera

abdopublishing.com

Published by Abdo Zoom™, PO Box 398166, Minneapolis, Minnesota 55439. Copyright © 2018 by Abdo Consulting Group, Inc. International copyrights reserved in all countries. No part of this book may be reproduced in any form without written permission from the publisher. Abdo Zoom™ is a trademark and logo of Abdo Consulting Group, Inc.

Printed in the United States of America, North Mankato, Minnesota
022017
092017

THIS BOOK CONTAINS RECYCLED MATERIALS

Cover Photo: Andy Ryan/The Image Bank/Getty Images
Interior Photos: Andy Ryan/The Image Bank/Getty Images, 1; Shutterstock Images, 4–5, 8, 17; Salvagor Gali/iStockphoto, 6–7; Lakeview Images/Shutterstock Images, 9; iStockphoto, 10, 11, 16; Aaron Nystrom/iStockphoto, 13; Tōhoku Japanese Earthquake sculpture by Luke Jerram, 14–15; William J. Smith/AP Images, 19; Gary Hincks/Science Source, 21

Editor: Brienna Rossiter
Series Designer: Madeline Berger
Art Direction: Dorothy Toth

Publisher's Cataloging-in-Publication Data
Names: Rivera, Andrea, author.
Title: Earthquakes / by Andrea Rivera.
Description: Minneapolis, MN : Abdo Zoom, 2018. | Series: Natural disasters | Includes bibliographical references and index.
Identifiers: LCCN 2017930342 | ISBN 9781532120374 (lib. bdg.) | ISBN 9781614797487 (ebook) | ISBN 9781614798040 (Read-to-me ebook)
Subjects: LCSH: Earthquakes--Juvenile literature.
Classification: DDC 363.34/95--dc23
LC record available at http://lccn.loc.gov/2017930342

Table of Contents

Science

Earthquakes shake the ground.

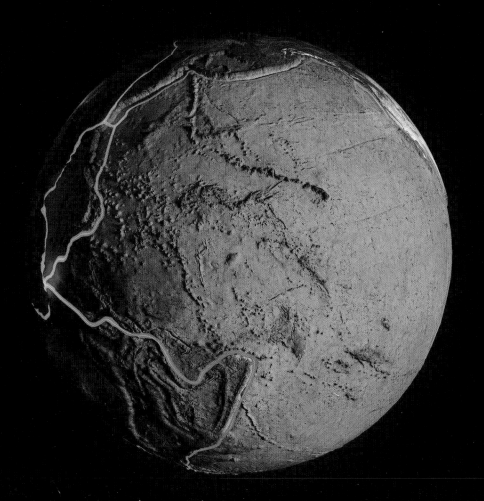

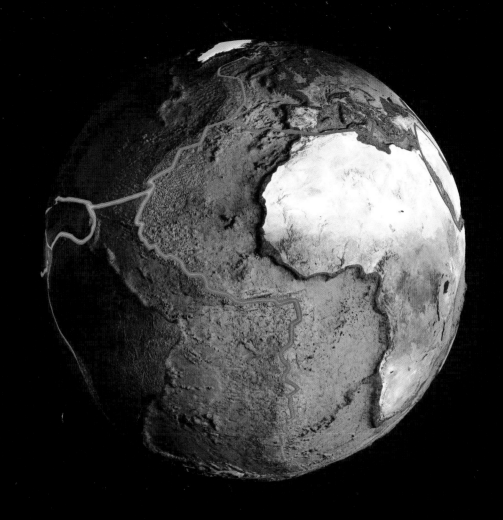

They happen when Earth's **crust** shifts. The crust is made of pieces called **plates**.

The plates move slowly.
Sometimes their edges get stuck.
Energy builds up.

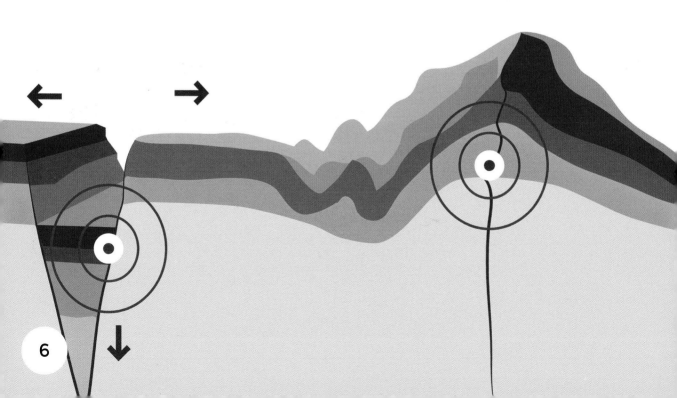

6

When the edges
break apart, the
energy is let out.
It shakes and cracks
the ground.

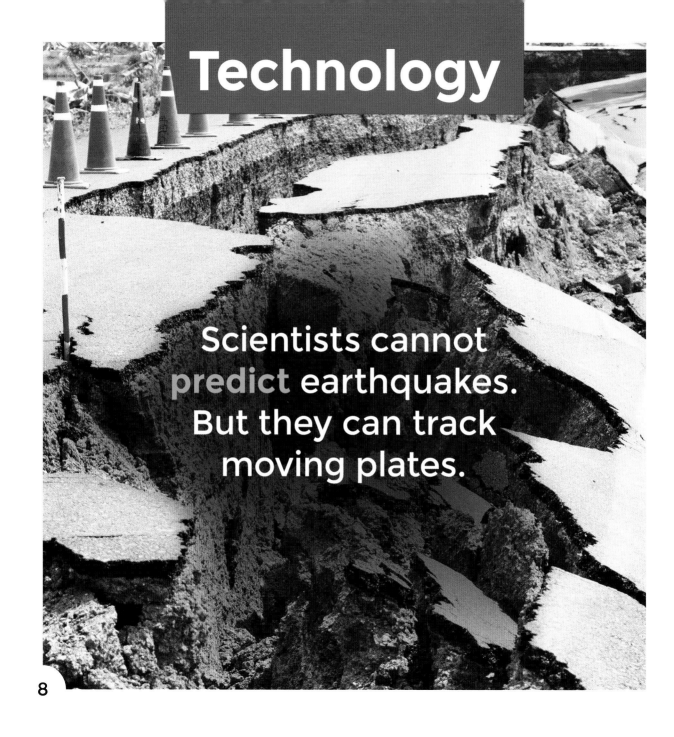

Technology

Scientists cannot **predict** earthquakes. But they can track moving plates.

They use special tools.
The tools help them know
what happens underground.

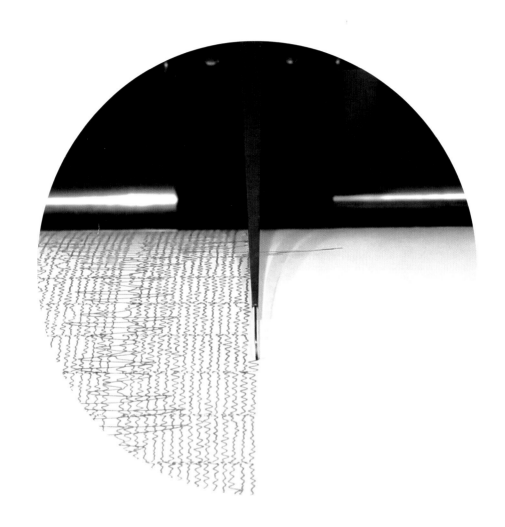

They use seismographs, too.

These tools show an earthquake's strength. They also show where it started.

Engineering

Engineers study how buildings react to earthquakes. They make safer buildings. Some new buildings can bend. They will not break when an earthquake shakes them.

Art

Luke Jerram made a sculpture. It looks like **seismic waves** from an earthquake. Jerram used a computer.

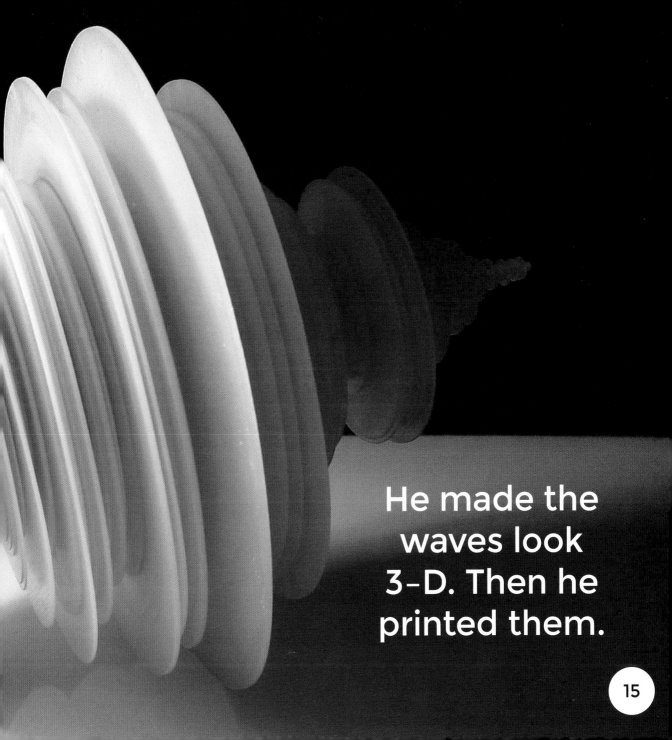

He made the waves look 3-D. Then he printed them.

A scale uses numbers to show an earthquake's strength.

Earthquakes rated below 5.0 will not cause much harm. Earthquakes rated above 7.0 are very dangerous.

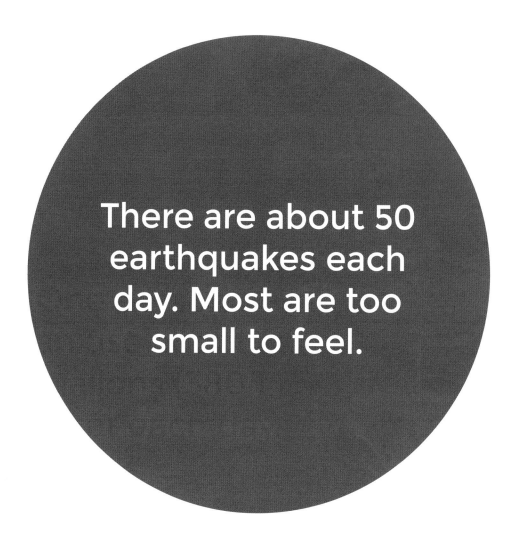

There are about 50 earthquakes each day. Most are too small to feel.

The strongest recorded earthquake was a 9.5. It was in Chile in 1960.

Key Stats

- About 80 percent of earthquakes happen along the Ring of Fire. This area goes around the Pacific Ocean.

- Most earthquakes last for a few seconds. Big ones may last for 10 to 30 seconds.

- The longest-lasting earthquake was on December 26, 2004. It lasted more than eight minutes!

- Earthquakes often cause other natural disasters. They can cause avalanches, landslides, or tsunamis.

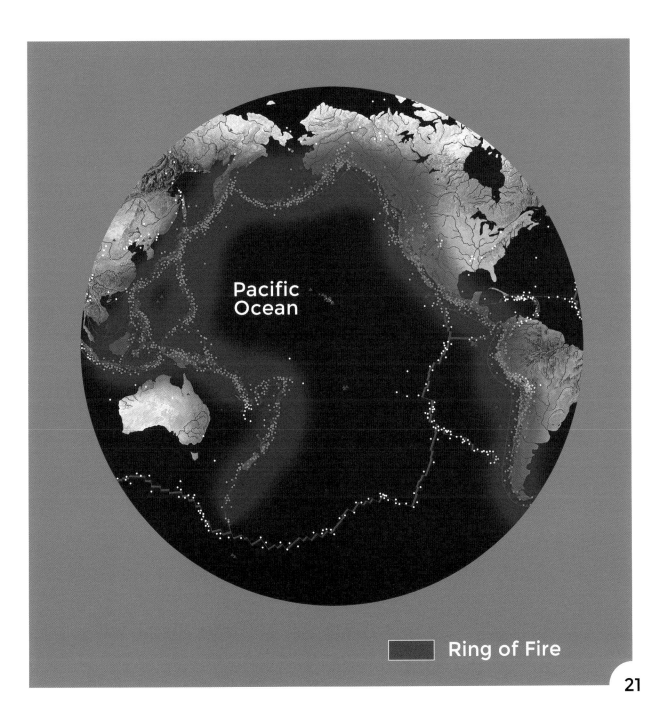

Pacific
Ocean

Ring of Fire

Glossary

crust - the hard outer covering of a planet.

plate - a large, moveable piece of Earth's crust.

predict - to guess what might happen in the future.

seismic wave - a wave of energy released by an earthquake.

seismograph - a tool that measures an earthquake's movement.

Booklinks

For more information on earthquakes, please visit abdobooklinks.com

 In on STEAM!

Learn even more with the Abdo Zoom STEAM database. Check out abdozoom.com for more information.

Index